S0-AFU-072

Chicago Public Library
Vodak/East Side Branch
3710 E. 106th St.
Chicago, IL 60617

Memorial Day

by Marc Tyler Nobleman

Content Adviser: Alton Hornsby Jr., Ph.D.,
Fuller E. Callaway Professor of History, Morehouse College, Atlanta, Georgia

Reading Adviser: Susan Kesselring, M.A., Literacy Educator,
Rosemount-Apple Valley-Eagan (Minnesota) School District

Let's See Library
Compass Point Books
Minneapolis, Minnesota

Compass Point Books
3109 West 50th Street, #115
Minneapolis, MN 55410

Visit Compass Point Books on the Internet at *www.compasspointbooks.com*
or e-mail your request to *custserv@compasspointbooks.com*

On the cover: Arlington National Cemetery in Arlington, Virginia

Photographs ©: EyeWire, cover, 4; Photodisc, 6; North Wind Picture Archives, 8; Justin Sullivan/Getty Images, 10; Image Ideas, 12; Tim Wright/Corbis, 14; Spencer Platt/Getty Images, 16; Comstock, 18; Robin Rudd/Unicorn Stock Photos, 20.

Creative Director: Terri Foley
Managing Editor: Catherine Neitge
Editor: Brenda Haugen
Photo Researcher: Marcie C. Spence
Designers: Melissa Kes and Les Tranby
Educational Consultant: Diane Smolinski

Library of Congress Cataloging-in-Publication Data
Nobleman, Marc Tyler.
  Memorial Day / by Marc Tyler Nobleman.
    p. cm. — (Let's see)
  Includes index.
ISBN 0-7565-0771-5 (Hardcover)
ISBN 0-7565-0953-X (Paperback)
1. Memorial Day—Juvenile literature. I. Title. II. Series.
E642.N63 2005
394.262—dc22   2004005089

Copyright © 2005 by Compass Point Books

All rights reserved. No part of this book may be reproduced without written permission from the publisher. The publisher takes no responsibility for the use of any of the materials or methods described in this book, nor for the products thereof.

Printed in the United States of America.

R0414249000

Table of Contents

Chicago Public Library
Vodak/East Side Branch
3710 E. 106th St.
Chicago, IL 60617

*NOTE: In this book, words that are defined in the glossary
are in* **bold** *the first time they appear in the text.*

MILFORD D ISAACSON
NATHANIEL THOMAS · DONALD R
KENNETH FRIERSON · BENJAMIN
ROBERT L JOHNSON · THOMAS J
DENNIS W SMITH · ROBERT
JAMES V VINCIGUERRA · VERNON M
PATRICK H HALBERT · RICHARD J
RAYMOND PLATERO · ROBERT
WILLIAM L WOOD · ERICK
PRESTON L HALL · EVERETT
THEODORE R LEIGHTON · JOSEPH V
ANTHONY B BATTEL
KENNETH E KOCH · JAMES F
JOHN J POLLACK · LEONARD
FRANK SPENCER III · ALLEN R TOWNER
OLIVER Y HARRELSON
ROBERT W SHELTON
NORMAN R EVERETT
BARRY V HOPPER
JEFF MILLER
GEORGE T SPILLERS
HARVIE R FRADY
DENNIS W MOORE
RICHARD WILLIAMS Jr
RICHARD A DORNELLAS
GREGORY L ANDERSON
PETER D GUZMAN
HOWARD BLANDINO
CHARLES T RUSSELL
JAMES C GRAFTON
GEORGE D QUICK Jr
RONALD C DAVIS · TERENCE
BARTHOLOMEW Jr
DEAN A

What Is Memorial Day?

Memorial Day is a holiday in the United States. On Memorial Day, people honor American men and women who died fighting for our country in a war. The war may have been big or small. It may have happened recently or long ago. The people who died in those wars are remembered at this time.

Some people get Memorial Day and **Veterans** Day mixed up. Both holidays honor men and women who were in the military. Veterans Day honors everyone who served in the military, both living and dead. Memorial Day honors people who have died in a war.

◄ *The Vietnam Veterans Memorial lists those who died in that war or are still missing.*

When Is Memorial Day?

Memorial Day falls on the last Monday in May every year. This gives many people a long weekend off from work or school.

Memorial Day is a national holiday. Schools are closed for Memorial Day. Many people do not have to work on this holiday.

◄ *Schools are closed on Memorial Day. Some schools are already out for the summer.*

How Did Memorial Day Begin?

After the **Civil War** (1861–1865), people felt the country should have a holiday honoring those who were killed. No one knows which town was the first to have Memorial Day. More than 20 U.S. towns say they started the holiday in the 1800s. Women in these towns put flowers on the graves of soldiers. They did that to honor those who had died trying to protect other people.

In 1866, Henry C. Welles helped start a Memorial Day **tradition** in Waterloo, New York. Two years later, General John A. Logan named May 30 as Memorial Day. Logan led a veterans group. Memorial Day became a national holiday.

◄ *People bury a soldier at a battlefield gravesite during the Civil War.*

How Do People Honor Soldiers on Memorial Day?

On Memorial Day, people fly the American flag at **half-staff** until noon. This shows respect for people who have died. At noon, the flag is raised to the top of the flagpole.

Many people go to cemeteries on Memorial Day and put flowers on soldiers' graves. Some place small American flags there. Some people wear **poppies** on their clothes to honor soldiers who died.

At 3 p.m., people stop for a moment of silence. They think about the brave men and women who fought in wars. Some may listen to "Taps." It is a slow military song played on a trumpet or **bugle.**

◄ *A boy looks at a gravesite flag on Memorial Day in San Francisco, California.*

What Else Do People Do on Memorial Day?

To some, Memorial Day marks the start of summer. They do not have to go to school or work. It is a day to spend with people in the community. Many meet with family and friends.

People enjoy the outdoors on Memorial Day. Many cities and towns have parades to honor soldiers. People have picnics and play sports. Many have cookouts or go to a beach. Some listen to patriotic music.

◀ *Children playing softball on Memorial Day*

Why Do Some States Have Two Memorial Days?

Memorial Day is a holiday in every state. Some states in the South also have another day like Memorial Day. On this second day, they remember soldiers from the South who died during the Civil War. It is often called **Confederate** Memorial Day.

This second Memorial Day is on different dates in different states. In Alabama, Mississippi, and Georgia, it is in April. In North Carolina, Virginia, and South Carolina, it is in May. In Texas, it is on January 19 and is called Confederate Heroes Day. In Tennessee, it is on June 3 and is called Confederate Decoration Day. It is also on June 3 in Louisiana.

◄ *Actors march through Richmond, Virginia, to honor Confederate soldiers.*

How Has Memorial Day Changed?

At first, Memorial Day was called Decoration Day. It got this name because it was a day when people decorated graves with flowers. In 1882, the name changed to Memorial Day. People wanted the holiday to focus on the soldiers, not the graves.

Memorial Day began to honor soldiers from the Civil War. After World War I, people began to honor soldiers from all wars on Memorial Day. In addition, the holiday has become a time for people to honor family and friends who have died.

Memorial Day was on May 30 every year. In 1971, Congress made Memorial Day fall on the last Monday of May.

◄ *Veterans march in the Memorial Day parade in Brooklyn, New York.*

Why Do Some People Want to Change the Holiday's Date?

Some people are not happy that Congress changed the date of Memorial Day. They want the holiday to always be on May 30.

Congress changed Memorial Day so it would be part of a three-day weekend. People can go away with their families or friends for a longer time.

Some people say this is not the real meaning of Memorial Day. They think it is more important to remember soldiers on Memorial Day than to take a vacation. They feel that if the holiday is the same date every year, people will remember the real reason for Memorial Day.

◄ *Families often go on picnics or vacations during Memorial Day weekend.*

What Does Memorial Day Mean to People?

Memorial Day is a serious day. It is a time when Americans are thankful they live in a free country. They think about the men and women who were killed in battle. Those soldiers died so the United States could stay free. Soldiers were not strangers to everyone. They were someone's friends and relatives.

Today, Memorial Day is also a happy day. People celebrate freedom in many ways. They spend time with other people, talking and laughing. They know they can do these things because others have fought to keep them free.

◄ *People take part in Memorial Day activities at a cemetery in Tennessee.*

Glossary

Civil War—a war from 1861 to 1865 between the Northern and Southern states; the North won

bugle—a musical instrument that looks like a small trumpet

Confederate—a soldier who fought for the South in the American Civil War

half-staff—halfway up a flagpole; on ships, flags are flown at half-mast

poppies—flowers

tradition—a custom that is common among a family or group

veterans—people who served in the military

Did You Know?

✶ In 1966, the U.S. government named Waterloo, New York, the official birthplace of Memorial Day. Other American cities and towns still claim they had Memorial Day first.

✶ Some U.S. cities along the ocean have a special way of honoring soldiers who died when they were at sea. People in these cities fill tiny ships with flowers. Then they put the ships in the water on Memorial Day.

✶ On the first national Memorial Day in 1868, General James Garfield, a Civil War hero and future president, made a speech at Arlington National Cemetery in Virginia. Afterward, 5,000 people helped decorate the graves of 20,000 soldiers.

✶ In some places, Boy Scouts and Girl Scouts put flags, flowers, or candles at the graves of soldiers on the Saturday before Memorial Day.

Want to Know More?

At the Library

Ansary, Mir Tamim. *Memorial Day.*
    Des Plaines, Ill.: Heinemann Library, 1999.
Cotton, Jacqueline S. *Memorial Day.*
    New York: Children's Press, 2002.
Frost, Helen. *Memorial Day.* Mankato,
    Minn.: Pebble Books, 2000.
Nelson, Robin. *Memorial Day.* Minneapolis:
    Lerner Publications Co., 2003.

On the Web

For more information on *Memorial Day,*
use FactHound to track down Web sites
related to this book.

1. Go to *www.facthound.com*
2. Type in a search word related to this
   book or this book ID: 0756507715.
3. Click on the *Fetch It* button.

Your trusty FactHound will fetch the best
Web sites for you!

On the Road

Arlington National Cemetery
Arlington, VA 22211
703/607-8000
To visit the national cemetery, exhibits,
and bookstore

The Waterloo Memorial Day Museum
35 E. Main St.
Waterloo, NY 13165
315/539-9611
To see a mansion filled with items about
Memorial Day and the time of the Civil War

Index

About the Author

Marc Tyler Nobleman has written more than 40 books for young readers. He has also written for a History Channel show called "The Great American History Quiz" and for several children's magazines including *Nickelodeon*, *Highlights for Children*, and *Read* (a Weekly Reader publication). He is also a cartoonist, and his single panels have appeared in more than 100 magazines internationally. He lives in Connecticut.